# Other books by Author

... more will be revealed soon...

# WAR WITHIN

## WW II:
## THIS MY CELL

VOLUME 2 OF 7

# MICHAEL R. BANE

WestBow
PRESS®
A DIVISION OF THOMAS NELSON
& ZONDERVAN

WestBow Press books may be ordered through booksellers or by contacting:

WestBow Press
A Division of Thomas Nelson & Zondervan
1663 Liberty Drive
Bloomington, IN 47403
www.westbowpress.com
844-714-3454

All Scripture quotations are taken from the King James Version.

ISBN: 978-1-6642-3612-7 (sc)
ISBN: 978-1-6642-3613-4 (e)

Print information available on the last page.

WestBow Press rev. date: 06/22/2021

# CONTENTS

## Chapter 1  Human Clay

## Chapter 2  Colors

## Chapter 3  Eye for an Eye

## Chapter 4  My Prison

## Chapter 5  Mirror, Mirror

## Chapter 6  Misery

## Chapter 7   Forgiveness

# DEDICATION

I dedicate this volume to my daughter Cheré René Bane. I remember that day, the day she was born. I learned more about love that day, then in all the years before, and after of my whole life.

And though we spent many days apart, the days that I have spent with her since, are some of my most special moments.

I look forward to so many more, and with her children, my grandchildren, I learned to love even more.

Cheré, I want you to know you are so special, and you are loved.

I can't promise to be there for the rest of your life

But I can promise to love you,

For the rest of mine.

Dad

# INTRO WW II

I am so excited, as I come close to
Finishing this, my second collection of writings.
So many years, and so many faces, and those
memories have surfaced during this time.
I actually felt my spirit being fed as well
Some of the topic matter is quite deep.
But my true belief is that each poem is
meant for someone, my greatest desire
for constructing this edition, is that, that someone
is you, each page is meant only to help, and not hurt.
This war is real. God be with you ...

# CHAPTER 1

## HUMAN CLAY

Genesis 1:27

So God created man in His own image,
In the image of God created He him,
Male, and female created He, him.

KJV

# WHEN IT WAS WRITTEN

# TURNS TO DUST

There is a time for everything
everything has it's time
To have control, is to do
everything in it's time.
We can not rush things,
things take time.
things of worth are worth the time
time alone, quiet time
there is no beginning, or end to time
there is always time to dream
time to close your eyes
and hope for better days
Time to listen, time to love
when we choose to share our time
with others, that is love,
change takes time
Time is all we truly have.
Everything else turns to dust
It's what we do with our time
that makes us who we are ...

# MUD

There is something
really wrong with me
I think, I might be insane

I feel like there is
ice in my heart, and
mud in my veins

Is it too late?
is this the end
of all things?

Am I insane?
is there something
really wrong with me?

Or, is it ok to have
ice in your heart, and
mud in your veins?

# THE MIRY CLAY

I think about the depths from where I came
and I thank you, Lord.
You pulled me out of the miry clay
and I am free.
So, now I must not look back
I will keep my eyes on the prize.
The chains fell from my hands and feet
you lifted me
and, I am free.
I will walk forward
and, not look back.
Everything has changed, and became new
my love, and my hope grows.

And each day, I am closer to you
and further from where I came
that day you pulled me out of the mirery clay
and I will not look back.
My spirit is new, because of you
you, live in me.
and everything has changed
I will keep my eyes on you
and no matter what
I will not look back.
that is what I hear you say:
Don't look back ...

# TORN

ripped to pieces
torn in two
torn apart
me and you
we were one
now were two -

# TEARS

My tears cannot compare
my tears of joy
my tears of sorrow
my tears of pain
can not compare
My tears of salt, and water
can not compare
to your tears
your tears of blood...

# DRY BONES

Nothing is colder
than dry bones.
If you are alive, but
your soul is dead
then your bones are dry
and you are cold.

You will never be warmed
goodness can not reach you

The sun cannot reach your
dead soul, or
warm your dry bones

# PONDER ON THIS

We have all heard the story
of the wolf in sheep's clothing

But what about the sheep
Who is in wolves clothing?

Pause for a moment, and
ponder on this notion.

Can you make sense of
this sentiment?

The wolf in sheep's clothing
is out to deceive.

Where the sheep in wolves clothing
can not be deceived.

So your trickery
will not work on me

For I am His sheep
ponder on this, a moment

# CHAPTER 2

## COLORS

Genesis 37:3b

And he made him a coat of many colors.

KJV

# WHEN IT WAS WRITTEN

# MR. WINTER

Mr. Winter
the respect you demand.
Mother nature has nothing on you
you are cold and calculating,
not much different than a killer.
In fact you are ... Mr Winter.
Green turns to brown
almost dead, clinging to life
at your mercy, your victim.
Brown turns to white
Mr. Winter
you show your beauty
but so much death.
Mr. Winter
you even turn liquid into solid
nothing less than a mad scientist.
You may feel I'm being hard on you
Mr. Winter ...
But, thats because you are so hard on me
I can not wait til spring
and if I survive again
I will forgive again
Until then, Good-bye
Good-bye Mr. Winter

# SHADES OF GRAY

Life is not all dark, and white
its full of shades of gray.
One point there's a stormy night
and then a sun filled day.
Sometimes its hard to balance life
with work and rest and play.
And realize things that come along
won't always go our way.
From the mountain tops, to the city block
to the wide open plains.
Some people bring us happiness
and others bring us pain.
One little boy will cry
because, His day was ruined by rain.
But what about the farmer?
God answered all his prayin.
Why must one man break his back
to bring his hard earned pay?
and another just sit and relax
and only use his brain?
Most things that come along
are usually shades of gray.
And sometimes, things get better
if we hang on one more day.

# NEW BLUE

New blue
nothing is the same
all is new
when I dream out loud
or am I awake?
Breathing while asleep
ice crosses
Falling from the sky
which is up? New blue
white raven
dark sunrise
nothing is the same
silent thoughts
the words not formed
a breath away floods the sky
Where is this place?
New blue

# PEACEFUL GLIMPSES

Silent screams, violent whispers
woken dreams, peaceful glimpses
groosum flowers
beautiful disaster
a lighted soul, a wicked master
underwater skies
honest lies, darkened angels
wingless flies
colorless rainbows, white darkness
dark clearity, peaceful glimpses

# THE COLOR REMAINS

What is this I feel?
a dull, aching pain

A push, a pull
the skin it stains

the pain is gone
but the color remains

To express who I am
what I've became

the stories I tell
the expressions it told

you must look close
as it all unfolds

the ink, and the needle
it helps me to feel

the pain is gone
but, the color remains

# CHAPTER 3

# EYE FOR AN EYE

Ecclesiastes 2:14a

The wise mans eyes are in his head,
but the fool walketh in darkness.

KJV

# WHEN IT WAS WRITTEN

# DON'T CLOSE YOUR EYES

Don't close your eyes to the pain inside
Everybody hurts, everybody cries.
We must learn to live this life
through the pain, through the strife.
Share who we are, all the pain inside
Everybody hurts, everybody tries.
We only have so much time
your days are numbered, so are mine.
So don't close your eyes to the love inside
share it with others, now is the time.
Keep your eyes open, don't be blind
to all the wonderful things in this life.
Everybody hurts, everybody dies
so lets make the best of it
and don't close your eyes.

# IN THE EYE OF THE STORM

As thunder, and lightning crashes around
and I am in the eye of the storm
and can see no relief in sight.
I close my eyes, and wait for better days
and as the hope grows to faith
and faith turns to love
the clouds begin to move,
and the eye of the storm disappears
and love fills the sky,
and as I feel this love, and hold this love
I can pass it on to others
and share what I've been through
as I was alone in the eye of the storm.
You were never far away
you were there with me
in the eye of the storm.

# MY EYES

What do you see?
in my eyes
Do you see life?
Do you see hope?
When you look in my eyes
Do you see me?
Do you look right through?
Do you see you?
When you look,
in my eyes
Do you see death?
Do you see darkness?
Do you see light?
Do you see God?
in my eyes

What do you see?
Can you even look?
In my eyes
lift your head
open your spirit
open your mind
and look into my eyes.
the window to my soul
open to you
For you to see
Look deep -
Tell me what you see
in my eyes ...

# NEVER SEE ME

I've been changing, but
you'll never see me now

I'm so far away, and
you are where you are

And it doesn't even matter
who's to blame

I've been changing, but
you'll never see me now

You are where you are, and
I'm so far away

I've tried so hard
I've came so far

But you will never
See me now ...

# YOUR EYES

When I look into your eyes
I see hope

In your eyes
I see today is bright

When I look into your eyes
I see love

In your eyes
I see tomorrow

When I look into your eyes
I see a reflection of me

In your eyes
I see your soul, and mine

When I look into your eyes
I see a fire that can not be quenched

In your eyes
I see all this, and more

When I look into your eyes
I see always, and forever
In your eyes

# A STRANGER'S EYES

When you look into a stranger's eyes
tell me what you see ...
Do you see a friend, or foe
or something in between?
Do you see hope, or fear?
a nightmare, or a dream ...
But also you must realize
things aren't always what they seem ...
you never know from where he came
to make it through this far
For He could be an angel
who God sent to where you are ...

Or maybe there's a purpose
something you should do –
perhaps this person
could be helped by only you ...
Don't get me wrong
I'm not saying trust everyone you see
Some strangers are dangerous
Some strangers are mean ...
So I think with all these words I wrote
what I'm really trying to say
when you look into a strangers eyes
give that man a break ...

# CHAPTER 4

## MY PRISON

1 Peter 3:19

By which also he went and
preached unto the spirits in prison

KJV

# WHEN IT WAS WRITTEN

# STEEL & CEMENT

There is no love or warmth
in steel and cement.
Many days in my life
there I have spent.
the bars, the ceiling,
the walls, the floor.
the mesh on the windows
the locks on the door.
There is no fresh air
not even a breeze.
I can't smell the flowers
or see the trees.
I search for something
that will shed some light.
I reach for a bible
late in the night.
I read about Mathew,
John, Mark, Luke, and Paul.
But Jesus to me
was the most important of all.
My spirit was broken
to my knees I fell.
then Jesus was with me
right there in my cell.
He told me I'm forgiven
and that He loved me.
Ironic, I had to go there
to be free.

# WALL LESS

All alone in this wall less prison
the bars are not outside,
they are within.
All alone, with my own decisions
I try to scream
nothing comes out,
they are within.
the walls are too thick
the walls are too high
they are not outside,
they are within.
No scream comes out,
they are within.

# MAKE BELIEVE

I live in my own mind
of make believe
I'll give you a peek
Do you like what you see?
or will you run?
are you afraid of me?
Just take a look
but don't be deceived
nothing is what
it appears to be.
Welcome to my mind
of make believe
But I also must warn you
once you enter
you can never leave
you are trapped in my
mind of make believe.

# BREAK

Take this confusion
runnin around my mind
I don't feel real any more
I am an illusion
Something happened in my brain
Is it a contusion?
Can you help me, find me?
Who I used to be
cause I don't feel real anymore
am I an illusion?
Something happened, I need you
Why this confusion?
Is this a heart break,
or a break down?
I don't feel real anymore
can you help me understand?
Is this a heart break,
or a break down?

# THE JAGGED TRIANGLE

The jagged triangle
my thoughts, so strange
I search for that light
darkness, I find
the quiet, the still
Why must you elude me?
I escaped you once
and now you return
I must let you go
but your grip is so tight
my time is almost over
that day is near
the jagged triangle
if only just a glimpse
I take the journey
and only I can go,
to face all I am, and was
will I be turned away?
because of this darkness
this thing, that is not mine
will you let go?
the jagged triangle
must soon become two

# STOP LIVING ALONE

Have you ever felt helpless, afraid, and in doubt?
and sure that things would never work out?
the helpless feelings, alone, and in tears
and pain bottled up over the years
not knowing that others felt the same
all the guilt, all the shame
Its time to realize, there's a better way
stop living alone, stop running away
and learn to share, and learn to give
learn to love, and learn to live
the time is now, to start today
stop living alone, stop running away
Don't turn back now, you've come too far
Share what you feel, share who you are
take your time, take it slow
the time is now, it's time to grow
stop running away, stop living alone.

# WHO AM I?

What kind of man am I? Look into my eyes.
Search deep inside. Deep into my eyes
to my very soul, my cell
Tell me please who do you see?
Can you tell me my identity?
When I stare into the looking glass
I'm all confused, I see my past
Not my present, or my future
But days gone by, like a clouded sky, overcast.
So what kind of man am I?
I must ask myself, because you do not know me,
Not like I know me, I can lie to you
But to myself I can not lie
I have to tell the truth.
And if you look into my eyes
you may catch just a glimpse of who I am.
If I open up, and let you in, in my cell.
Now, what kind of man am I?
A lonely man, a man alone?
an angry man, a heart of stone?
or a confused child, who has not grown?
trying to love, but was not shown.
Again, what kind of man am I?
would you please tell me what's inside?

# CHAPTER 5

# MIRROR, MIRROR

James 1:23, 24

For if any be a hearer of the word, and not a doer, he is like unto a man beholding his natural face in a glass: For he beholdeth himself, and goeth his way, and straightway forgeteth what manner of man he was.

KJV

# WHEN IT WAS WRITTEN

# MY MIRROR

I look at you
its me I see

that's why I hate you
because I hate me

I try to look through you
it does not work

I try to avoid you
but you're always there

you are a reflection of me
your eyes, my mirror

you scare me
I'm frightened

So, I run away
I run fast, I run far

I get there, and
there you are

I'm not running from you
I'm running from me

I can't get away
what must I do?

I know I better surrender
you are my mirror

that's why I hate you
because I hate me.

# WOULD YOU?

Tell me would you give a minute
to a stranger?
to listen to him
and give him directions?

Tell me would you give an hour
for an acquaintance?
to help him bare
his load?

Tell me, would you give a day
to a friend?
to help her
in her need?

Tell me, would you give your life
for a brother?
Would you give your life
for a friend?
Would you give your life
for a stranger?

Would you do what Jesus did for me?
Would you do what Jesus did for you?
Could you?
Would you do what Jesus did?

# YOURSELF

Show yourself
be yourself
reveal yourself
unmask yourself

Only you can be yourself
be yourself
love yourself
unmask yourself

# WHEN I SEARCH

I search my soul
I search my mind
I search my heart
see what I find
the more I search
the more I see
I see things
so differently
when I search myself
when I search me
the change is there
its plain to see
the more I search
the more I see
when I search myself
when I search me
I see my God
From up above
I see His ways
I see His love
the more I search
the more I see
and through His love
I learn
to love me

# TOO LATE

It's not too late to change my mind
to search myself
see what's inside
to search within, to change my life
to search my heart
to search my soul
the time is now before its too late
to change my mind
to change my fate
to search my heart, to search my soul
to learn to live
to learn to grow
Its not too late there still is time
to search myself
see what I find
Its not too late, there still is hope
to change my heart
to mind my soul
the time is now, before its too late
to learn to love
and not to hate
the time is now, its not too late.

# WHO I AM?

When I look at me
Who do I see? Who am I?

Am I someone who helps, and not hurts?
Am I someone who cares?
or am I cold?

Do I gossip, or back-bite?
Do I always cause problems?
or do I spread love, and peace?
and leave you happier than I found you

Who am I?
What do I see? When I look at me.

Am I full of pride with an ego ready to explode?
or am I meek, quiet, and humble?
Do I lie, cheat, and steal?
or am I honest, upright, and just?

Do I judge, or condemn you?
or do I accept you, respect you?
Am I better than you? Do I think I know it all?
or am I teachable, willing and eager to learn?
and also willing and able to teach.

Who am I? What do I see?
When I look at me.

Do I realize you are God's child?
and you are in my life, not by chance
but for a reason, the reason may be
unknown now, but it is there.

So when I look at you
I must look at you through God's eyes
then I can love you, unconditionally
expecting nothing in return.

This is what I see, when I look at me.
This is who I am.

# CHAPTER 6

## MISERY

1 Corinthians 12:26a

And whether one member suffer,
all the members suffer with it.

KJV

# WHEN IT WAS WRITTEN

# MISERY

Misery loves company
that is what they say

But I believe it is a choice
to live in peace, or stay...

With misery comes fear
selfishness, and pain

Loneliness, and torment
alone I go insane ...

But I believe I have a choice
its there for me to find

To listen, and to hear
to open up my mind ...

Now misery let go of me
I choose to live, let go!

You no longer have a grip on me
I choose to live, to grow ...

So now I say good-bye to you
Good-bye misery

Today I have choices
You no longer live in me ...

So now I say Good-bye to you
Good-bye misery

After all it is my choice
and I choose to be free ...

# CUT

As the blood flows through the vein
and the cut releases pain...
and the cloud becomes rain
then I know the angels cry
and the seed becomes a bloom
and a spark becomes a flame
as if its just a game
nothing is the same
and everything will change
in a moment I'm insane
when I cut against the grain ...
and all my fluids drained
the angels cry, it rains
and the cut releases pain...

# SWEET CATASTROPHE

Why did he slip, rip?
Why was his wrist slit?

He was a product of the system
a sweet catastrophe

Everyone looked, but
no one could see ...

Why didn't he tell you?
He tried

The times he opened up,
and cried ...

Everyone looked, but
no one could see

He was a product of the system
a sweet catastrophe ...

# ME, MY MURDERER

So many people cry ...
So many people die
this is war
me, my murderer
I kill myself by my mistakes
by the drugs I take
It was not always this way
I am to blame
this is a war I cannot win
I kill myself, me, my murderer
so many people die
so many people cry ...
if you are not like me
you can not understand these things
But you do understand
the lives it changed
and the pain it brings

by my mistakes
by the drugs I take
So many lives changed
So many families rearranged
If you are not like me
you can not understand such things
But you can understand
the pain it brings.
By my mistakes, by the drugs I take
I kill myself, me my murderer
so many people cry ...

# AT WAR WITH ME

Hate me today
hate me tomorrow
if that's what it takes
For you to love you
So, I'm at war with me
hate me today
if that's what it takes
for you to love you
So, do whatever it takes
For you to leave me behind
just leave me here
at war with me
the most important thing to me
is that you, love you ...

# MISTAKE

All the mistakes you made
staring at the sharp blade
please remember things can change ...
I can help you
every choice you make
every cut you chase
every scar you claim
please let me help you ...
you are not a mistake

# CHAPTER 7

# FORGIVENESS

Psalms 32:1

Blessed is the man whose transgression
is forgiven, whose sin is covered.

KJV

# WHEN IT WAS WRITTEN

# PRODIGAL SON

Many days in my life I was tempted
Many lusts of the flesh, I fell to these.
Now I come back to you Father, broken hearted
Now I come back to you Father, on my knees.
And, He tells me welcome home son, your forgiven,
and He tells me welcome home son, you are clean.
and He tells me welcome home son, I still love you
even more than the first day you believed.

Now I come back to you Father
Now I come back to you Father
Now I come back broken hearted, on my knees

Many days in your life when you were tempted
Many lusts of the flesh, you fell to these
Now come back to your Father, broken hearted
Now come back to your Father, on your knees.
And He'll tell you welcome home son, your forgiven,
and He'll tell you welcome home son, you are clean.
And He'll tell you welcome home son, I still love you,
even more than the first day you believed.

So now come back to your Father
come back to your Father
Now come back to your Father broken hearted, on your knees

Now we come back broken hearted on our knees...

# NEW LIFE

My new life starts now
every day a new beginning
more acceptance, and learning.
My new life starts now
it is a process, not a destination.
I must give my all today
without hesitation.
My new life starts now
filled with decisions
keeping alive my dreams, my visions
My new life starts now
Yesterday's mistakes, are gone, forgiven
Everyday, I have what I need
to live victorious, to succeed
my new life starts now ...

# THE MIRACLE

You are a miracle, I am to.
just look at the things that God
has brought us through
So, now its time to give ourselves a chance
To search deep within, more than a glance
to forgive ourselves for the things
we have done.
to learn that we don't have to run.
and to know that we are worth good things
we can accomplish our goals
and live out our dreams,
and it all comes when we realize
that now is the time
to stop wasting our lives,
and, to live in the miracle, in victory
Now is the time, for you, and for me ...

# AS DARKNESS TURNS TO LIGHT

As night turns into morning
and darkness turns to light
I have another opportunity
to choose to do what's right.

I set aside a moment
to talk to God above
I thank Him for His grace
His faithfulness, His love

He gives me strength to do the things
that I must do today
to get through any obstacle
that might be in my way

Its nice to know that God is there
that I am not alone
as I continue on this journey
down this long, and winding road.

As night turns into morning
and darkness turns to light
each day I must surrender
I no longer have to fight

As hope turns into faith
my God is always near
just knowing that I'm not alone
I no longer live in fear

Now anything is possible
my futures looking bright
each day now holds new meaning
as darkness turns to light.

# WHAT I LEFT BEHIND

I know what ever
it is I find
it will be much better
than what I left behind

I know that when I
seek His face
what I will truly find
is grace

I know that when
He arrives
I will be with Him
that very day.

I know that I must
wait til then
even though I don't
know when

I just know that
what I find
will be so much better
than what I left behind ...

# THERE WITH ME

Weather I'm in a deep valley
or the very tip of the highest mountain
you are there with me ...
weather I'm home alone, or
many miles from nowhere
I know you are there ...
From the dryness of the desert
to the depths of the sea
you are there with me ...
there is nowhere I can go, ever
where you were not there before
During the darkest times in my life
as well as my brightest days
I know you are there ...
It doesn't matter where I've been
It doesn't matter where I go
and when I get to wherever I go
I know you will be
there with me ...

Printed in the United States
by Baker & Taylor Publisher Services